THE UGLY FACE OF UNCONTROLLED

ANGER

The Effects of Anger on the Human Body

Avoiding Situations That Cause You to Lose Your Temper

Learning to Control Your Anger

KENNETH DADZIE

Encourages All People To Control Their Anger
Irrespective Of The Circumstances And Thereby
Avoid The Unpleasant Situations Associated With
Uncontrolled Anger

THE UGLY FACE OF UNCONTROLLED ANGER

The effect of anger on the human body
Avoiding situations that cause you to lose your temper
Learning to control your anger

Kenneth Dadzie

HCU Media LLC
Accra, Ghana ◇ Frisco, TX

THE UGLY FACE OF UNCONTROLLED ANGER

A study in Christian Life Principals

HCU Media LLC

Published and Copyright © 2020 by Kenneth Dadzie & HCU Media LLC

ISBN-13: 978-1-939468-15-4 (Paperback Edition)

Also available in Kindle edition

Printed in the USA

Scripture quotations, unless otherwise noted, are from The Holy Bible,
New King James Version, Personal Study Edition © 1995, Thomas Nelson
Publishers, Nashville, TN USA

Cover Design by Dale Henry – www.dalehenrydesign.com

December 2020
10 9 8 7 6 5 4 3 2 1

TABLE OF CONTENTS

The Ugly Face of uncontrolled anger

DEDICATION

To all people who desire to control their anger in all situations of life.

SPECIAL THANKS

Kenneth & Magdalene Dadzie
One*flesh*, One Mind, Determined to Control Our Anger
I express my sincere and heartfelt appreciation to my beloved wife, Magdalene Dadzie who has been standing and continues to stand by me in my ministry.

PREFACE

Anger is an emotional capacity given to man by God. It plays both positive and negative roles in a man's life. However, the challenge of how to control our anger is a problem all of us struggle with. Anger is a boomerang. It always comes back to you, sometimes with serious consequences. Research has shown that anger has serious repercussions on the human body. Kenneth Dadzie in this book **"The Ugly Face of Uncontrolled Anger"** has encouraged all people to control their anger and offered suggestions that will assist all people to control their anger and thereby avoid the unpleasant situations associated with uncontrolled anger.

ACKNOWLEDGEMENTS

Anger is an emotional capacity given to man by God. It plays both positive and negative roles in a man's life. However, the challenge of how to control our anger is a problem all of us struggle with. Anger is a boomerang. It always comes back to you, sometimes with serious consequences. Research has shown that anger has serious repercussions on the human body. I intend to present materials that will encourage all people to control their anger and thereby avoid the unpleasant situations associated with uncontrolled anger.

The materials in this book are part of a sermon presentation I made at the Kweikuma Church of Christ. I have intentionally prepared the lesson in a very simple form for easy study and to enable those who will like to use them for group discussions and classroom presentation to do so. The reader may find some of the materials in the book overlapping. This is not intentional since I did not initially prepare the materials for publication in this form.

I express my sincere and heartfelt gratitude first and foremost to God the Almighty for the wisdom and the ability given me to write this book. Secondly, to the leaders and all the members of the Kweikuma Church of Christ for their interest, encouragement and support that made it possible for this sermon to be presented in the church and other congregations as well. I express my profound gratitude to Dr. Alexander Ekow Asmah for his encouragement and for his untiring efforts that made the publication of this book possible.

I shall forever remain indebted to the Gomoa Tarkwa Church of Christ for nurturing me in the Lord, Mr. Theophilus N. D. Brandford-Arthur, former Personnel Manager of Paper Conversion Company (PCC) Ltd,

Takoradi and Dr. Tawiah Siameh of Effia-Nkwanta Regional Hospital, Takoradi who read through the manuscript and offered suggestions. I am also indebted to Bro. Edward Yeboah-Acquah, Emmanuel Nuako and the late Joseph Baah for their special interest in the early days of my ministry and many others who have shown love and concern for me in my ministry.

In spite of the painstaking effort that has been made to correct omissions and errors, it is possible that there may be omissions and errors. I am responsible for such omissions and errors. I do not claim originality to all the ideas presented here. Like most preachers, I have had access to very good books, sermon notes, and articles of preachers and writers and heard other preachers speak on this topic. I am grateful to all those I have quoted and to all who have influenced me in one way or the other.

My prayer is that this book will encourage all people to control their anger and thereby avoid the unpleasant situations associated with uncontrolled anger. If this is done, I hope to have achieved my aim.

INTRODUCTION

Life in our day can be described as "hustle and bustle" and as a result many are on the verge of an emotional explosion. Christians are not exempted from the havoc of uncontrolled emotions. We have our fair share of anger, fear, depression, guilt, low self-esteem and other emotional problems. One emotional problem that many seem not to have control over is anger. Uncontrolled anger has led to so many unpleasant situations; confusion, chaos, anarchy and terrible consequences.

The Scriptures state, *"So Esau hated Jacob because of the blessing with which his father blessed him, and Esau said in his heart, the days of mourning for my father are at hand then I will kill my brother Jacob. And the words of Esau her older son was told to Rebekah. So she sent and called Jacob her younger son and said to him, surely your brother Esau comforts himself concerning you by intending to kill you. Now therefore, my son, obey my voice; arise, flee to my brother Laban in Haran. And stay with him a few days, until your brother's fury turns away, until your brother's anger turns away from you and he forgets what you have done to him; then I will send and bring you from there. Why should I be bereaved also of you both in one day?"* (Italics and emphasis KD).[1]

"On the seventh day, when the heart of the king was merry with wine, he commanded...seven eunuchs who served in the presence of king Ahasuerus to bring Queen Vashti before the king wearing her royal crown, in order to show her beauty to the people and the officials, for she was beautiful to behold. But Queen Vashti refused to come at the king's command brought by the eunuchs; therefore the

---

[1] Genesis 27:41-45

king was furious and his anger burned within him. Then the king said to the wise men who understood the times…What shall we do to Queen Vashti according to law, because she did not obey the command of king Ahasuerus brought to her by the eunuchs…Then Memucan answered before the king and the princes…If it pleases the king, let a royal decree go out from him …that Vashti shall no more come before king Ahasuerus and let the king give her royal position to another who is better than she…And the reply pleased the king and the princes and the king did according to the word of Memucan…After these things when the wrath of king Ahasuerus subsided, he remembered Vashti, what she has done, and what has been decreed against her," (Italics and emphasis KD). [2]

"A certain man had two sons. And the younger of them said to his father, father, give me the portion of goods that falls to me. So he divided to them his livelihood. And not many days after, the younger son gathered all together journeyed to a far country and there wasted his possessions with prodigal living. But when he had spent all…he arose and came to his father. But when he was still a great way off, his father saw him and had compassion, and ran and fell on his neck and kissed him. And the son said to him, father, I have sinned against heaven and before you and no longer worthy to be called your son. But the father said to his servants, bring out the best robe and put it on him…And they began to make merry. Now his older son was in the field. And he came and drew near to the house, he heard music and dancing. So he called one of the servants and asked what these things meant. And he said to him, your brother has come, and because he has received him safe

---

[2] Esther 1:10-2:1

and sound, your father has killed the fatted calf. But he was angry and would not go in. Therefore his father came out and pleaded with him." (Italics and emphasis KD).[3]

All the above passages indicate the terrible consequences of uncontrolled anger. Therefore, the Scriptural admonition, ***"Be angry, and do not sin, do not let the sun go down on your wrath, nor give place to the devil,"*** (Italics and emphasis KD)[4] deserves our consideration. The Scriptures encourage all of us to control our anger and thereby avoid being manipulated by Satan when we lose our temper.

I intend to present the Scriptural approach on how we can control our anger. We shall discuss practical and usable suggestions for thinking and acting right. It is based upon the belief that, God through His word has given us all things that pertain to life and godliness (2 Peter 1:3).

Just as God gave some animals the power to protect themselves by speed, colour, odour, horns, quills, etc., He gave man the power to become angry for self-protection. A man's anger may indicate his displeasure about certain situations. Notwithstanding, He expects us to control our anger in order to avoid being manipulated by Satan and other resultant consequences. In order to help us to control our anger, let us first understand anger.

---

[3] Luke 15:11-28
[4] Ephesians 4:26

CHAPTER ONE: ANGER DEFINED

WHAT IS ANGER?

Anger is an emotional capacity given to man by God. It plays both positive and negative roles in a man's life. It is **a strong feeling caused by being insulted, hurt, robbed etc., that makes you want to hurt a person, have revenge, be unpleasant etc.**[1]

The challenge of how to control our anger is a problem all of us struggle with. Anger is a boomerang; it always comes back to you, sometimes with serious consequences. Therefore, control your anger before it hurts you. Research has shown that anger has serious repercussions on the human body.

ANGER AND THE HUMAN BODY

Anger is irrational and when you are angry, you do not have the full complement of your senses, hence there is a tendency to behave unreasonably. Medical experts have concluded that the human body has been structured in a way that it responds to external stimuli such as light, sound, touch, etc., and internal stimuli such as anger, joy, bitterness, love and jealousy. Anger is an internal stimulus and it is believed that most psychiatric problems are associated with people who are not able to manage internal stimuli. Therefore, manage your anger before it manages you.

---

[1] Personal Notes

Anger has direct and indirect effect on the human body. When one becomes angry his adrenal glands (two small organs above one's kidneys that produce adrenalin) secret violence poison into the blood stream and one flares up. The poison can cause one to be ill for a day or two. It has been revealed that anger can let some people have anorexia (loss of appetite). Anger can cause peptic ulcer (a small painful area inside one's stomach). This is because, anger may cause an imbalance in the autonomic nervous system, resulting in increased vagal stimulation of gastric secretion causing the ulcer. Anger is a precipitating factor for convulsion, epilepsy and asthma.

Anger increases the body's need for cortical hormones to be able to adjust to the new situation of the body. Inability or inadequate secretion of adrenocorticotropic hormones from the pituitary glands results in adrenalin insufficiency (lack of a chemical produced by one's adrenal glands that makes the heart beat faster and gives additional energy when one is frightened, excited, or angry). This is manifested by depression and may lead to Addison's disease (a serious ailment of the cortex of the adrenal glands). Anger has a link with the destruction of the beta cells of the pancreas which is responsible for the production of insulin (a hormone which regulates the blood sugar level) thereby causing Diabetes Mellitus.

Dr. S. I. McMillen, a renowned medical Doctor stated, *"Fatal heart attacks can be triggered by anger in all degrees and anxiety,"* (Italics and emphasis KD).[2]

---

[2] Dr. S. I. McMillen, None of These Diseases, Fleming H. Revel, Grand Rapids, MI, USA

G. M. Trevelyan said, *"Anger is a momentary madness, so control your passion or it will control you,"* (Italics and emphasis KD).[3]

Mark Twain described anger as, *"An acid that can do more harm to the vessel in which it is stored than to anything on which it is poured,"* (Italics and emphasis KD).[4]

Alfred A. Montapert says, *"Every time you get angry, you poison your own system,"* (Italics and emphasis KD).[5]

Garrison Keillor says, *"A man can't eat anger for breakfast and sleep with it at night and not suffer damage to his soul,"* (Italics and emphasis KD).[6]

Though the power to become angry is a God given attribute, the Scriptures' admonition to us to control our anger is in the right direction because of its effects on our physical bodies and its spiritual consequences.

---

[3]https://www.brainyquote.com (G. M. Trevelyan, an English historian, 1876-1962)
[4] Ibid (Mark Twain, an American author and humorist, 1835-1910)
[5]https://www.branyquote.com (Alfred A. Montapert, an American author and philosopher, 1906)
[6] Ibid (Garrison Keillor, an American author, humorist and radio personality, 1942)

CHAPTER TWO: SCRIPTURE & ANGER

THE SCRIPTURES WARN US
AGAINST UNCONTROLLED ANGER

The Scriptures strongly warn us against uncontrolled anger. They state, *"Cease from anger, and forsake wrath. Do not fret, it only causes harm,"* (Italics and emphasis KD).[1]

"A quick-tempered man acts foolishly," (Italics and emphasis KD).[2] *"... I say to you that whoever is angry with his brother without a cause shall be in danger of the judgment,"* (Italics and emphasis KD).[3]

"... now you yourself are to put off all these: anger, wrath, malice, blasphemy, filthy language out of your mouth," (Italics and emphasis KD).[4] *"So then, my beloved brethren, let every man be swift to hear, slow to speak, slow to wrath,"* (Italics and emphasis KD).[5]

As stated earlier, uncontrolled anger has led to so many unpleasant situations and brought untold hardships. Cain killed his brother because of his uncontrolled anger (Genesis 4:5-6). Nebuchadnezzar put Shadrach, Meshach and Abed-Nego into fire because of uncontrolled anger (Daniel 3:13). Haman plotted to exterminate the Jews as a result of his anger against Mordecai (Esther 3:3). Herod ordered the children of Bethlehem to be slaughtered in his anger (Matthew 2:16).

---

[1] Psalm 37:8
[2] Proverbs 14:7
[3] Matthew 5:22
[4] Colossians 3:8
[5] James 1:19

When one allows his or her anger to carry over into another day it may develop into inward hate and bitterness that may easily lead to a heart which can be used by the devil for evil works. Peter stated, *"Be sober, be vigilant; because your adversary the devil walks about like a roaring lion, seeking whom he may devour. Resist him, be steadfast in the faith, knowing that the same sufferings are experienced by your brotherhood in the world,"* (Italics and emphasis KD).[6]

THE SCRIPTURES ENCOURAGE US
TO CONTROL OUR ANGER

The Scriptures admonish all of us to control our anger irrespective of the circumstances. They state that, *"He who is slow to anger is better than the mighty. And he who rules his spirit than he who takes a city,"* (Italics and emphasis KD). [7]

 "The discretion of a man makes him slow to anger. And his glory is to overlook a transgression," (Italics and emphasis KD). [8]

 "Do not hasten in your spirit to be angry, for anger rests in the bosom of fools," (Italics and emphasis KD)[.9] *"A soft answer turns away wrath, but a harsh word stirs up anger,"* (Italics and emphasis KD). [10]

 "He who is slow to wrath has great understanding, but he who is impulsive exalts folly," (Italics and emphasis KD). [11]

---

[6] 1 Peter 5:8-9
[7] Proverbs 16:32
[8] Proverbs 19:11
[9] Ecclesiastes 7:9
[10] Proverbs 15:1
[11] Proverbs 14:29

"A wrathful man stirs up strife, but he who is slow to anger allays contention." (Italics and emphasis KD). *[12]* *"Make no friendship with an angry man and with a furious man do not go."* (Italics and emphasis KD). *[13]*

---

[12] Proverbs 15:18
[13] Proverbs 22:24

CHAPTER THREE: CONTROLLING ANGER

NINE STEPS TO CONTROL YOUR ANGER

1. Avoid Situations That Cause You To Lose Your Temper

Make every effort to take note of situations that cause you to lose your temper and avoid them. Remember you cannot control the actions and speech of others, but you can control how you react to them.

Brain researchers have found out that when people are scared, hurt or angry, stress hormones flood their bodies and this results in the shutting down of the rational part of their brain. When the irrational part of the brain takes over, that is not the time to try to have meaningful discussions with them. Angry people don't discuss, they rant and rave.

Whenever you notice that you are uncomfortable with anyone because of anger, go away for a short time and come back after you have calmed down. While you are away, ponder on your behaviour and figure out how you can move from defending yourself to resolving the problem.

Benjamin Franklin said, *"Whatever is begun in anger ends in shame,"* (Italics and emphasis KD). [1] Thomas Paine noted, *"The greatest remedy for anger is delay,"* (Italics and emphasis KD).[2] Joseph Joubert was of the opinion that, *"The best remedy for a short temper is a long walk,"* (Italics and emphasis KD).[3]

---

[1] https://www.brainyquote.com (Benjamin Franklin, an American founding father, 1706-1790)
[2] Ibid (Thomas Paine, an English-American politician and author, 1737-1809)
[3] Ibid (Joseph Joubert, a French writer, 1754-1824)

2. Do Not Hold On To Your Anger

Gautama Buddha stated that, *"Holding on to anger is like grasping a hot coal with the intent of throwing it at someone else; you are the one who gets burned,"* (Italics and emphasis KD).[4]

Holding on to your anger is like a pressure cooker; sooner or later the lid will blow off. If you hold on to your anger it will lead you to become bitter. Anger and bitterness are the most obvious reaction when there is a conflict and these are often shown in facial expressions, words or actions. But remember, words said in anger are very harmful and are difficult to be taken back, so control your anger before it controls you.

The Bible acknowledges anger as a human weakness, nonetheless, you need to manage it with care otherwise it could ruin your nurtured relationship. The Scriptures state, *"Be angry, and do not sin; do not let the sun go down on your wrath, nor give place to the devil,"* (Italics and emphasis KD).[5]

"But if you have bitter envy and self-seeking in your hearts, do not boast and lie against the truth. This wisdom does not descend from above, but is earthly, sensual, demonic, for where envy and self-seeking exist, confusion and every evil thing are there," (Italics and emphasis KD).[6]

There are three things you should not do when you lose your temper and become angry. **Firstly**, do not let your anger lead you into sin. **Secondly**, do not prolong your anger. **Thirdly**, do not let your anger give a foothold to the devil. All of the above three are possible if you are not able to control your anger.

---

[4] Ibid (Gautama Buddha, founder of Buddhism, 563-483 BC)
[5] Ephesians 4:26-27
[6] James 3:14-16

3. Avoid Hot-Tempered People

To enable you to control your anger, avoid hot-tempered people for they destroy families and relationships. The Scriptures state, ***"Make no friendship with an angry man, and with a furious man do not go, lest you learn his ways and set a snare for your souls,"*** (Italics and emphasis KD).[7]

Hot-tempered people destroy brethren but long-tempered people keep them together. As Christians, the Scriptures admonish us to be patient with other people. We are taught to "forebear" each other (Ephesians 4:2). In simple terms, this means "to put up with" those things we do not like about others. When we are patient with those we love, we quickly make excuses for their mistakes. However, those we do not love can do nothing to please us.

4. Resolve To Solve Your Differences

In spite of your feelings about the one you perceived to be the cause of your anger, the ideal thing to do after taking up the issue with God in prayer is to talk with the offender alone first and resolve to solve your differences.

Meet in private and discuss the matter just between the two of you. Keep your conflict and the resolving process quiet away from curious ears and eyes. You both listen and try to understand each other's reasoning and feelings. Listen to the perceived offender with your ears, eyes, mind and heart and understand his or her point of view.

Even if the offense led to you being at loggerheads, it is necessary to meet the person face to face because you will be in a better position to express yourselves better and analyse the circumstances together. After personally meeting the perceived offender and dealing with the issue, it is

---

[7] Proverbs 22:24-25

important not to talk about it again. If the issue is successfully resolved in private, it must be kept as such (Matthew 18:15). With this approach you both grow in love and self-sacrifice by putting the other's needs first (Philippians 2:1-4).

5. Alter Any Situation That Causes You To Lose Your Temper By Being Assertive

Don't be passive about whatever caused you to lose your temper which led to your frosty relationship but be assertive to resolve the issue with the person you perceived to be the offender. However, in every corrective measure which is initiated to resolve an issue of offense, the end result must be to reconcile people to God.

This requires looking at the offense with eyes of love like Jesus did. A judgmental attitude alienates people from God and makes reconciliation difficult. It also tends to make the offender more defensive and further aggravates the frosty relationship between the offender and the offended. Therefore, in doing so remember to set a Christian example.

6. Adapt To Situations That Cause You To Lose Your Temper By Focusing On The Bigger Picture

Relationships are based on mutual respect. When someone offends you or when there is a conflict in any relationship, it is important to create a healthy balance between detesting the offense and loving the offender. It is okay to express contempt for the offense or to admonish the offender, whichever comes first, it is important to address the problem but not to attack each other.

It is therefore very important to sometimes compromise by adjusting your standard and focus on the positive. This will help you to strengthen yourself and look at the bigger picture. Joseph looked at the bigger picture, the future of the family when he decided to forgive his brothers irrespective of what had happened (Genesis 50:15-21).

7. Accept Situations You Cannot Change That Cause You To Lose Your Temper By Letting Them Go

As difficult as it may be, remember that there are some things you cannot change about people who have relationship with you hence the Scriptures' admonition that, *"If it possible, as far as it depends on you, live at peace with everyone,"* (Italics & emphasis KD)[8]. Martin Luther stated that, *"You cannot keep birds from flying over your head but you can keep them from building a nest in your hair,"* (Italics & emphasis KD).[9]

Therefore, accept the things you cannot change about those who have relationship with you especially if they are your family members and let go of any differences. However, you must also remember that the situation can change when you look up to God for the needed change (2 Corinthians 4:8-9; 1 Peter 5:7-11).

8. Learn To Forgive Those Who offend You

The Scriptures enjoin us to be ready and quick to forgive those who offend us. Jesus stated, *"Take heed to yourselves. If your brother sins against you, rebuke him, and if he repents, forgive him. And if he sins against you seven times in a day, and seven times in a day returns to you saying I repent, you shall forgive him,"* (Italics and emphasis KD).[10]

---

[8] Romans 12:18, NIV
[9] https://www.goodreads.com (Martin Luther, a German Professor of theology and priest, 1483-1546)
[10] Luke 17:3-4

Forgiveness is changing of one's inappropriate thoughts and attitude toward the event that is past. However, man has always struggled with forgiveness. It is one of the hardest things for a person to do. One of the greatest difficulties of life is to win over an unforgiving spirit especially if it has been held in the heart over many years.

All of us need to learn how to forgive others. Jesus came to teach mankind about forgiveness. He came both to forgive and to tell us we need to forgive. He never withheld forgiveness from anyone who sincerely asked for it (Matthew 18:21-35). If we are willing to follow the principle Jesus taught and lived, we would be amazed at the drastic change in the number of problems we would have with one another (Ephesians 4:30-32).

A willingness to forgive is very important, not only for the sake of the person being forgiven but for our own sakes as well. As the spirit of forgiveness is cultivated, we come to realize more and more that we are as often in need of being forgiven. People will be quick to overlook our faults and give us an opportunity to correct them only if we show this attitude in dealing with others. Paul Stated, ***"Do not be deceived, God is not mocked; for whatever a man sows, that he will also reap,"*** (Italics and emphasis KD).[11]

Forgiveness is one of the basic characteristics of those who are in the church. It has so many blessings and benefits for mankind; spiritual, social and personal. It is an absolute necessity if our relationship with God is to be proper. Jesus warns, ***"Therefore if you bring your gift to the altar, and there remember that your brother has something against you, leave your gift there before the altar, and go your way. First be reconciled to your brother, and then come and***

---

[11] Galatians 6:7

offer your gift," (Italics and emphasis KD).[12] Forgiveness must be the controlling attitude in our lives. We cannot be truly what God wants us to be unless we develop the spirit of forgiveness.

9. Pray For God's Help

Pray for help and wisdom from God as you try to control your anger. James admonished, *"If any of you lacks wisdom, let him ask of God, who gives to all liberally and without reproach and it will be given to him,"* (Italics and emphasis KD).[13]

This is probably the most important rule of all. Even after you have followed all the other steps, you can still fail to control your anger if you do not remember to pray. Remember a Christian's greatest weapon is payer. Jesus stated, *"Watch and pray, lest you enter into temptation,"* (Italics and emphasis KD).[14]

Do not let a day go by without praying to God, asking Him to help you control your anger. The Lord will help you to control your anger if you remember to pray.

---

[12] Matthew 5:23-24
[13] James 1:5
[14] Matthew 26:41

CHAPTER FOUR: CONCLUSION

How you handle your anger says a lot about what sort of person you are. Anger is like a fire, when handled appropriately, it can bring great good. But out of control, it can destroy people's lives (Genesis 49:6-7).

Once anger is recognised, one should act on it, instead of harbouring it to fester and become destructive (Psalm 4:4). Whether good or bad, anger is powerful, so it needs to be controlled. Solomon wrote, ***"Wrath is cruel and anger a torrent." "An angry man stirs up strife, and a furious man abounds in transgression,"*** (Italics and emphasis KD).[1]

Uncontrolled anger is dangerous and should be avoided. A Christian's strong weapon against anger is self-control. This means that we must have proper control of our temper, for the Scripture says ***"Be angry, and do not sin; do not let the sun go down on your wrath, nor give place to the devil,"*** (Italics and emphasis KD).[2]

---

[1] Proverbs 27:4; 29:22
[2] Ephesians 4:26-27

THE AUTHOR

Kenneth Dadzie is a Minister of Kweikuma Church of Christ, an Author, Marriage and HIV/AIDS Counselor and a former Health Services Administrator, Ateiku Christian Hospital, Ateiku. He has been a church leader for thirty-eight (38) years, preached for twenty-six (26) years and taught New Testament Greek, Hermeneutics and Apocalyptic Literature for sixteen (16) years. He has preached and also served as a resource person on religious discussion programs on local radio stations from 2002–2020.

He holds a Bachelor of Arts (Biblical Studies) degree from the Theological University of America (TUA), Iowa, USA, Advance Diploma (Biblical Studies) and Diploma (Biblical Studies) from the International Bible Institute (IBI) Bellville, South Africa, Diploma in English Language and Business Administration from the Writers Bureau College of Business, Manchester, England and Certificate (Health Administration & Management) from the GIMPA Public Services School (GPSS), Accra Ghana.

He was honoured as a distinguished graduate and personality of the month of November 2014 for his contribution in equipping the saints for the work of the ministry by the Theological University of America. He is married to Magdalene Dadzie and they have five children and six grandchildren. You can reach him on phone: 0276139293/0547919159 or email him at ken.dadzie@gmail.com.

OTHER BOOKS TO BE PUBLISHED BY THE AUTHOR

DON'T PUT ASUNDER
(A SIMPLIFIED HANDBOOK FOR PRE-MARRIAGE COUNSELING)

BASIC COUNSELING SKILLS

GETTING ACQUAINTED

KNOWING YOUR PARTNER

UNDERSTANDING MARRIAGE

HANDLING CONFLICTS IN A GODLY WAY

LIVING WITH YOUR IN-LAWS

PREPARING FOR YOUR MARRIAGE

CHRISTIAN MINISTERS HANDBOOK
(A PRACTICAL GUIDE FOR SPECIAL OCCASIONS)

SOLEMNIZATION OF HOLY MATRIMONY

CUSTOMARY MARRIAGE RITES

FUNERAL SERVICES & WIDOWHOOD RITES

NAMING CEREMONY

THANKSGIVING SERVICES

BIRTHDAY CELEBRATION

CELEBRATION OF WEDDING ANNIVERSARY

ORDINATION OF ELDERS & DEACONS

WHO WE ARE
HCU Media LLC

Publishing in support of

Heritage Christian University – Ghana (HCU Ghana)

www.hcuc.edu.gh

HCU media has been established to support the publication of materials, both paper and electronic, created by faculty and friends of HCU Ghana. These materials will be offered initially in the USA & Ghana but may become available globally via other outlets.

Made in the USA
Columbia, SC
14 December 2023

27884059R00024